LIVING GREEN
SAVING OUR EARTH

Patricia Clare

The Rosen Publishing Group's
PowerKids Press™
New York

Published in 2009 by The Rosen Publishing Group, Inc.
29 East 21st Street, New York, NY 10010

Book Design: Haley Wilson

Photo Credits: Cover, p. 17 © prism_68/Shutterstock; pp. 4–5 © Zacarias Pereira da Mata/Shutterstock;
p. 6 © Natalie Fobes/Science Faction/Getty Images; p. 6 (ducks) © Jed Jacobsohn/Getty Images;
p. 9 © Alexey Samarin/Shutterstock; p. 10 © Svetlana Privezentseva/Shutterstock; p. 12 © Mr. B Hughes/
Shutterstock; p. 13 © Ulrike Hammerich/Shutterstock; p. 14 © JustASC/Shutterstock; p. 15 © Stephen Finn/
Shutterstock; p. 18 © Sherri R Camp/Shutterstock; p. 21 © Andrew Chambers/Shutterstock.

Library of Congress Cataloging-in-Publication Data

Clare, Patricia, 1972-
  Living green : saving our earth / Patricia Clare.
      p. cm. — (Real life readers)
  Includes index.
  ISBN 978-1-4358-2968-8 (library binding)
  ISBN: 978-1-4358-0121-9
  6-pack ISBN: 978-1-4358-0122-6
  1. Green movement—Juvenile literature. 2. Conservation of natural resources—Juvenile literature. 3.
Environmental protection—Citizen participation—Juvenile literature. I. Title.
  GE195.5.C63 2009
  333.72—dc22

                                    2008036887

Manufactured in the United States of America

Contents

What Does Living Green Mean?   4

Water Pollution   7

Air Pollution and Global Warming   8

Fighting Land Pollution   15

More Ways to Live Green   20

Glossary   23

Index   24

What Does Living Green Mean?

Have you ever heard someone talk about "living green"? People have been using this term a lot more in everyday life. "Living green" means making choices that help Earth and our **environment**.

These oil factories allow their waste to mix with the air around them. Pollution in air and water can travel to distant places, too.

Human actions are changing our world in harmful ways. Rain forests are being cut down for wood and farmland. Wild animals are dying out as their homes are destroyed to make room for cities. Pollution is in our air, land, and water. Many people believe that it's time to start "living green." It's time to change our world in good ways.

ducks covered in oil

In 1989, a ship off the coast of Alaska spilled almost 11 million gallons (42 millon liters) of oil. Many plants and animals died in this polluted water.

Water Pollution

People who live green fight three main kinds of pollution: water, air, and land pollution. Water pollution can kill plants, fish, and other animals. We may get sick if we eat fish or drink water from polluted areas.

Oil spills and trash dumping are some kinds of water pollution. Other forms include harmful **chemicals** used to grow plants, which may mix with nearby bodies of water. Land pollution, such as household cleaners, sometimes ends up in our water, too.

Living green means not adding to any kind of water pollution. It also means using less water because it takes a lot of power to make our water clean.

Air Pollution and Global Warming

People who live green are also worried about air pollution. Chemicals in the air can harm people as well as plants and animals.

The burning of **fossil fuels** such as coal, oil, and natural gas causes some air pollution. We've been burning these fuels in great amounts to create power for our homes, cars, and businesses. When fossil fuels burn, they put out **greenhouse gases** that build up in the air surrounding Earth. The gases trap too much of the sun's heat on Earth and cause Earth's overall **temperature** to rise. This rise in temperature is called global warming.

Air pollution can lead to trouble breathing and serious illnesses.

This glacier in Norway is melting because of global warming.

Does global warming affect you? You'd be surprised how many ways it does. For example, warmer temperatures affect the weather. Hot weather can create dangerous storms, such as **tornadoes**, that can harm communities.

Did you know that most of the world's freshwater comes from **glaciers**? We need freshwater to drink and grow crops, but many glaciers are melting in warmer temperatures. Water from the melting glaciers flows into the oceans' salt water, so we have less freshwater to use. Also, melting glaciers raise sea levels, which can harm animals, plants, and people who make their homes on coasts.

People who live green try to slow global warming by using fewer fossil fuels. For example, they walk or ride their bikes instead of driving to cut down on the greenhouse gases that cars make. People can buy cars that run on cleaner kinds of power, too.

These machines use wind instead of fossil fuels to create electricity.

People can also use power from **natural resources** other than coal, oil, and gas. Natural resources, such as sunlight, plants, water, and wind, provide clean power and won't run out. However, it takes Earth millions of years to make fossil fuels, and we've been using them in great amounts at a very quick rate.

This building uses the sun's rays for power. Some of the "windows" on this house are actually tools that collect the sun's energy.

Some kinds of waste, such as the bottles shown here, can be recycled into something new. For example, a recycled bottle could be turned into a toy.

Fighting Land Pollution

Recycling is one way that people have been trying to stop land pollution. When we recycle, objects that have been used are remade into something else. Recycling cuts down on the amount of waste and trash we make. It also uses less power and resources than making products from fresh natural resources.

Cans and bottles take a long time to turn back into soil. It's better to recycle them so they can be broken down and made into new cans and bottles or something else. Paper can be broken down and remade into more paper. This helps save trees from being cut down to make paper.

Reducing is another way to stop land pollution. Reducing means making less waste. If you throw out your paper lunch bag each day, you'll have thrown out almost 200 paper bags by the end of the school year! However, if you use the same lunch bag over and over, you'll have reduced the amount of paper you use.

You can reduce the amount of power that you use in your daily life by turning lights off when you leave a room. You can put on a sweater rather than turning up the heat. Can you think of other ways that you can reduce?

Trash dumps are getting larger as people throw out
their old objects.

At a yard sale, people find objects that can be reused rather than buying new ones.

Another important part of living green is reusing resources. Like recycling and reducing, reusing prevents more land waste. You can refill bottles of water. You can use empty food tubs for art projects. You can give your toys and games to someone who wants them rather than throwing them away. Did you know that you can make blankets from scraps of clothes? Things that you don't want anymore may be just what someone else wants!

Three Ways to Live Green		
word	**meaning**	**examples**
recycle	to change something so that it can be used again	follow your community's recycling plan
reduce	to use less of something	use less paper and less electricity
reuse	to use something again without changing it	use a bottle or can again; give away a toy

More Ways to Live Green

There are other things you and your friends can do to "live green." You can take your own cloth bags to a store so you don't bring home bags that you'll throw out. You can also write your government leaders and ask them to make laws to stop pollution.

Buying food that is grown near you is living green, too. This food does not need to be driven long distances to the store. A short drive reduces the amount of greenhouse gases that are put into the air. You can even grow some of your own food!

Many people grow food in their yards or in a
community garden.

Pollution is a serious problem, but we do have ways to fight it.

Can you think of more ways to live green?

Problem:
Pollution helps cause global
warming and harms
the environment.

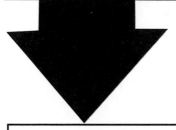

Ways to Solve It:
People can live green by:
- not littering;
- recycling, reducing, and reusing;
- using fossil fuels less;
- buying food grown nearby;
- asking government leaders to make laws.

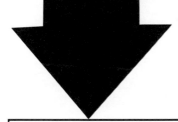

What Can Happen:
People will live on a cleaner,
healthier Earth.

Glossary

chemical (KEH-mih-kuhl) Matter that can be mixed with other matter to cause changes.

environment (ihn-VY-ruhn-muhnt) All living things and everything around them, including people, plants, and animals.

fossil fuel (FAH-suhl FYOOL) A supply of power, such as coal, natural gas, or oil, that is made from plants that died millions of years ago.

glacier (GLAY-shur) A large mass of ice that moves very slowly down a mountain or along a valley.

greenhouse gas (GREEN-hows GAS) A gas that traps heat near Earth's surface.

natural resource (NA-chuh-ruhl REE-sohrs) Something that can be found in nature and is used by people, such as wood, oil, or water.

temperature (TEHM-puhr-chur) How hot or cold something is.

tornado (tohr-NAY-doh) A storm with a funnel-shaped cloud and very powerful spinning wind.

Index

A
air pollution, 7, 8

B
buying food, 20, 22

C
change(ing) our world, 5
chemicals, 7, 8
choices, 4

E
environment, 4, 22

F
fossil fuels, 8, 12, 13, 22
freshwater, 11

G
glaciers, 11
global warming, 8, 11, 12, 22
government leaders, 20, 22
greenhouse gases, 8, 12, 20

L
land pollution, 7, 15, 16
laws, 20, 22

P
pollution, 5, 7, 20, 22
power, 7, 8, 12, 13, 15, 16

R
recycle(ing), 15, 19, 22
reduce(d), 16, 19
reducing, 16, 19, 22
reusing, 19, 22

S
sick, 7

W
water pollution, 7
weather, 11

Due to the changing nature of Internet links, The Rosen Publishing Group, Inc., has developed an online list of Web sites related to the subject of this book. This site is updated regularly. Please use this link to access the list: http://www.rcbmlinks.com/rlr/green